SPIRITUAL
INTERVIEW
WITH

BRUCE
LEE

THE RESURRECTION
OF THE
DRAGON

RYUHO OKAWA

HS PRESS

Contents

Preface

Now, here, he is. Famous "Dragon" came back. Who was he? What was he? And, now, where, why, how he is? Is it possible for him to be a dragon, even after his death? I mean "kung fu" or "Jeet Kune Do" can be understood in the realm of spirits, that is, without bodies.

In this book, Bruce Lee talked a lot about his philosophy. How could he use the word, "Fighting" compatible with "Peaceful Philosophy"?

Can "kung fu" be replaced by the words "Justice" "Love" "Peace" "Way" or "Buddha's Truth"?

Anyway, you can see "The Resurrection of the Dragon" in this book. And this fact will be the good news for the people of the world who still respecting Bruce Lee.

Ryuho Okawa
Master, Founder & CEO of Happy Science Group
Nov. 10, 2017

Spiritual Interview with Bruce Lee

The Resurrection of the Dragon

Recorded August 13, 2017
Special Lecture Hall, Happy Science,
Japan

Bruce Lee (1940~1973)

A martial artist and actor. His father was an actor in Hong Kong and was on tour in San Francisco, U.S. where Bruce Lee was born. Once returning to Hong Kong, he became a child actor in Hong Kong movies by the stage name Li Xiaolong. While enrolled at the University of Washington, he became fixated on martial arts which led him to creating his own original form of martial art, Jeet Kune Do. His fighting skills attracted Hollywood's attention and he became an action star in American TV shows. In 1971, he returned to Hong Kong to act in the movie, *Fists of Fury*. Afterward, he achieved his dream of acting in a Hollywood movie by starring in *Enter the Dragon*. However, he was bothered by severe headaches for an unknown reason and, in July 1973, right before the release of his movie, suddenly passed away. *Enter the Dragon* was a huge hit, and he became a worldwide star after his death.

Interviewers from Happy Science*:

Masayuki Isono
Executive Director
Chief of Overseas Missionary Work Promotion Office
Deputy Chief Secretary, First Secretarial Division
Religious Affairs Headquarters

Taishu Sakai
Special Assistant to the Chairperson
Religious Affairs Headquarters

Yuki Wada
General Manager, First Secretarial Division
General Manager of Overseas Missionary Work Promotion Office
Religious Affairs Headquarters

*Interviewers are listed in the order that they appear in the transcript. Their professional titles represent their positions at the time of the interview.

1

A Worldwide Star of Oriental Origin Returns After 44 Years

The riddle of his early death and His whereabouts in the other world

RYUHO OKAWA

Hello. We would like to summon the spirit of the famous Bruce Lee, the kung fu movie actor.

He is still famous worldwide. I knew him in my high school days, and he died in 1973. But after his death, he became famous through his movies. Even in Japan, a lot of his followers still respect him, especially people who are directing kung fu, martial arts or karate-like area, and actors and actresses. These people have deep, deep respect for him.

So today, we must investigate how he has been in the afterlife or spiritual world. When I wrote *The Mystical Laws*,[*] I wrote that the famous Bruce Lee might have dropped into not the heavenly world because I've heard from people that after his death, he appeared as a ghost and they said at that time, he smelled bad. In the context of Chinese tradition, how good they smell is very essential.

---

[*] See Chapter Four in *The Mystical Laws* (New York: IRH Press, 2015).

When they smell bad, it means the person is in Hell. But today, we are living in 2017, 44 years from his death. So, is his situation the same or not? We cannot be sure about it, so we want to check it.

But firstly, I must apologize to you. I cannot show the action of Bruce Lee in front of you because of my poor action now. So, it's difficult for me. It would mean my death, so I cannot.

Today's purpose is, we want to know the spirit of Jeet Kune Do. The founder is Bruce Lee. So, he has a philosophy regarding kung fu, especially *his* kung fu. Firstly, he was the disciple of famous Ip Man*, the grand master of Eishunken [Wing Chun] sector. Ip Man is very famous. Ip Man is Bruce Lee's *shifu* [fatherly master], but he was poor at making money and making the name of Eishunken prevail. Contrary to that, Bruce Lee was very good at making money [especially after his death] and he became famous in the world. So, through his famous movies, he became the hero of the movie world.

Here, I have several movies, for example, *The Big Boss*; this one is *Dragon Kiki Ippatsu* in Japanese [*laughs*]. *Fist of Fury*, or *Dragon Ikari no Tekken* [*laughs*], *The Way of the Dragon*, or *Doragon e no Michi*, *Game of Death*, or *Shibo Yugi*, and *Tower of Death*, or *Shibo no Tou* [see Figure 1].

---

* Ip Man (1893-1972) A master of Wing Chun. Born in Guangdong Province, China. He mastered Wing Chun, a traditional martial art in southern China. He spread Wing Chun in Hong Kong after WWII and developed his branch of Wing Chun, making it the largest in Hong Kong.

Young people are not familiar with Bruce Lee. [*While showing the Blu-ray disc cases.*] This is his face, what he looks like. I'm sorry I cannot show you something. If I'm Dragon Li Xiaolong, I can kick the ceiling of this room [*laughs*], [but I'm not,] so I'm very sorry about that.

He is an Oriental hero, even now

RYUHO OKAWA

OK. Is it enough on him? OK, OK, OK. I'll add an additional one.

He learned kung fu, but his original Jeet Kune Do

Figure 1.
Top left to right: *The Big Boss* (Golden Harvest, 1971), *Fist of Fury* (ibid, 1972), *The Way of the Dragon* (ibid, 1972).
Bottom left to right: *Game of Death* (ibid, 1978), *Tower of Death* (ibid, 1981), *Enter the Dragon* (ibid, 1973).

is quite different. Its concept is made up from a lot of martial arts, Judo, boxing or things like that. So, the form of Jeet Kune Do is quite contrary to that of common kung fu. His shifu, Ip Man, taught him Eishunken. It's some kind of defensive-type kung fu. But his Jeet Kune Do is an aggressive one. I think so. It seems like kickboxing or something like that.

He became famous through his movies, but to our regret, he died at the age of 32. He died too young. After his death, maybe *Moeyo Doragon* [*Enter the Dragon*] became famous in the world and he became a worldwide star. Before that, he appeared in the U.S. TV series, *Green Hornet*, as a karate actor for a character with a Japanese name, Kato, and became a great star.

His death is a riddle now. After his death, several movies regarding his life story were made, and even now, people know his famous, how do I say, dragon-bird-like voice, "Acho! Acho!" or [*laughs*] his nunchaku, so he really is the origin of the kung fu movie stars. We now have Jackie Chan, Jet Li or people like that, but he's the first one of the Oriental superstars, and was and is a hero of the Oriental world. I think so.

Then, I'll summon Bruce Lee.

He was born in the U.S.A., and of course, he had citizenship of the United States. But before the age of one, he returned to Hong Kong and in his younger days, he acted as a small movie star because his father was an actor of Hong Kong. After he became 19 years old, he entered the University of Washington and majored in philosophy, so his Jeet Kune Do kung fu has a philosophical aspect. He has pride in that aspect. So today, we must ask him about his philosophy and what he thinks of China, Hong Kong, Japan, or the U.S.A. This is today's subject. I think so.

I'm not sure if he can speak Japanese or not, but firstly, we'll start in English and then we can pursue his past life. Is it OK?

OK, then, famous actor Bruce Lee.
Would you come down here to Happy Science?
I am very sorry for making you wait three weeks.
You came to me
Before the Tokyo Dome lecture*,
But I let you wait more than three weeks.
I'm very sorry.
Would you please speak something for us?

[*About 10 seconds of silence.*]

---

* The author gave a grand lecture entitled "The Choice of Humankind" at Tokyo Dome on August 2, 2017.

Bruce Lee appears, showing off his moves

BRUCE LEE
[*Suddenly thrusts right hand forward, turns sideways and sticks up left index finger next to face, as if taking a Jeet Kune Do stance.*] Tou!!

MASAYUKI ISONO
Hello?

BRUCE LEE
Acho!

[*Interviewers laugh.*]

BRUCE LEE
[*While slowly making various hand movements.*] Oooh... Ko!

ISONO
Hello.

BRUCE LEE
Huh... Hello!

ISONO

Are you Mr. Bruce Lee?

BRUCE LEE

Sure. [*Performs a move.*] Ch! Chowaa...

ISONO

[*Laughs.*] Thank you for coming to Happy Science.

BRUCE LEE

What's Happy Science?

ISONO

"What's Happy Science?" We will explain it later, but...

BRUCE LEE

[*Shows many stances as if in an action scene, and takes a pose in the end.*]

ISONO

[*Laughs.*] Thank you. We are so happy to have you here.

BRUCE LEE

Uh-huh.

ISONO

We'd like to ask you several questions about your life in the other world.

BRUCE LEE

Uh-huh.

ISONO

And... [*Watches Bruce Lee act out Jeet Kune Do and nunchaku moves in his chair, but continues asking despite being interrupted.*]... about the philosophy of your... Jeet Kune Do and... current world issues.

BRUCE LEE

[*Preoccupied with his moves, he misses Isono's words*] Uh-huh. What?

ISONO

Sorry.

BRUCE LEE

What?

ISONO

We would like to ask you several questions.

BRUCE LEE
Several questions?

ISONO
Please teach us your philo...

BRUCE LEE
Teach you? What?

ISONO
Your thinking.

BRUCE LEE
Thinking?

ISONO
Yes.

BRUCE LEE
I'm thinking, yeah.

"I am still fighting"

ISONO

OK, so first of all, as Master Okawa explained earlier, just after you died, your ghost appeared and the smell was terribly bad. People used to say that you might have fallen down to Hell.

BRUCE LEE

[*Shuffling and looking at the Blu-ray disc cases of the movies starring himself.*] Hmm? Hell? No, no.

ISONO

Was it true?

BRUCE LEE

No! No, no, no.

ISONO

No, no?

BRUCE LEE

No. Completely no.

ISONO

So...

BRUCE LEE

[*Imitates the pose on the Blu-ray disc cover.*] Cho!

ISONO

[*Laughs.*] Where were you at that time?

BRUCE LEE

Hmm?

ISONO

Where were you right after you died?

BRUCE LEE

I'm fighting.

ISONO

You are fighting?

BRUCE LEE

Still fighting.

ISONO

You're still fighting?

BRUCE LEE

Hmm.

TAISHU SAKAI
Where do you live now?

BRUCE LEE
Hmm?

SAKAI
Live now?

BRUCE LEE
Hmm?

SAKAI
Where do you live now?

BRUCE LEE
Here.

ISONO
Here? Where? Where is "here"?

BRUCE LEE
Here.

ISONO
No, no, no.

BRUCE LEE
In front of you.

ISONO
No. Yes, we can see you, but you are now a spirit, so...

BRUCE LEE
[*Grunts as he shows his moves.*] Ho!

ISONO
OK, do you understand that you don't have a body of yours?

BRUCE LEE
No.

ISONO
No?

BRUCE LEE
No. I have a body with me.

ISONO
What kind of body do you have?

BRUCE LEE
Beautiful body.

ISONO
Beautiful body?

BRUCE LEE
Can I take off? [*Tries to take off jacket.*]

ISONO
No, no, no. Please don't, please don't.

BRUCE LEE
Oh. [*Sits back with a relaxed expression.*]

YUKI WADA
Who are you fighting?

BRUCE LEE
Hmm?

WADA
Who are you fighting?

BRUCE LEE
Enemy.

WADA
Who is your enemy?

BRUCE LEE

Devils. Devils, devils. Worldwide devils. Bad people of the world.

ISONO

Bad people? For example?

BRUCE LEE

Hmm? Mafia, gang, American racists, or Chinese evil politicians, like that.

ISONO

Evil politicians?

BRUCE LEE

[*Takes a Jeet Kune Do stance.*] Ocho! Ah...

ISONO

So, you are still in this world and fighting that kind of evil people?

BRUCE LEE

Are you good people?

ISONO

Yes, we are.

BRUCE LEE
[*Points to Sakai.*] He is questionable.

SAKAI
Good people, good people.

BRUCE LEE
Really?

SAKAI
Yes.

"My spirit is my body and my body is my spirit"

BRUCE LEE
Oh! Hmm... Hmm... OK. Oh, [*points to Wada*] you, beautiful lady.

WADA
Hello.

BRUCE LEE
Oh, Chinese? Or...?

WADA
My father is from Hong Kong.

BRUCE LEE

Hong Kong! Oh, yeah, good place.

WADA

He practices aikido and has a black belt.

BRUCE LEE

Oh, really?

WADA

So, he is a big fan of yours.

BRUCE LEE

[*Takes a fighting pose.*] Down! I want to fight him.

WADA

I think my father would lose against you. Actually, he is a very big fan. And... [*Bruce Lee stands up and throws a kick toward Isono with right leg.*] I think you are going to hurt yourself, so please sit down [*laughs*].

BRUCE LEE

OK.

SAKAI

Why did you come?

BRUCE LEE

Naked is beautiful [*gesturing his urge to take off jacket*].

WADA

The jacket you have on right now is beautiful.

SAKAI

Why did you come to our Master?

BRUCE LEE

Your Master?

SAKAI

Why?

BRUCE LEE

Ryuho Okawa is a kung fu master, so...

SAKAI

Kung fu master?

BRUCE LEE

I came here to fight with him. Ha! Grand master champion.

SAKAI

Do you understand that you are a spirit?

BRUCE LEE

Yeah. I'm a spirit and I have a body.

SAKAI

You have a body, even now?

BRUCE LEE

My spirit is my body. My body is my spirit. You know?

SAKAI

Yeah.

ISONO

Yes.

BRUCE LEE

My spirit is beautiful. My body is beautiful. Beauty... is myself.

2

Truth, Beauty, and Justice According to Bruce Lee

The spirit of Jeet Kune Do is the pursuit of the Truth

ISONO

OK. I'd like to ask about the spirit of Jeet Kune Do.

BRUCE LEE

[*Preoccupied with his moves, he misses Isono's words.*] Hmm?

ISONO

The spirit of Jeet Kune Do.

BRUCE LEE

Oh! The spirit of Jeet Kune Do is the pursuit of the Truth. You're also pursuing the Truth, Goodness, and Beauty. Me, too. Jeet Kune Do, too. All.

ISONO

OK. You often used to say that your motto is, "Honestly express yourself." So, my question is...

BRUCE LEE

[*While performing some moves.*] OK.

ISONO

Who are you? What are you?

BRUCE LEE

What? Hmm? Are you OK? Are you OK?

ISONO

Yes, I am OK.

BRUCE LEE

Do you have a problem in your brain?

ISONO

No, not at all.

BRUCE LEE

Oh, then it's OK.

ISONO

I asked because you said "to express yourself is your spirit or spirit of Jeet Kune Do." That's why I asked you, "Who do you think you are?" or "Who are you?"

BRUCE LEE

"Who are you?" It's a Zen mondo-like [*Zen dialogue-like*] question.

ISONO

Yeah, it's kind of like Zen-mondo, but you are a seeker of the Truth, so maybe you have an answer?

BRUCE LEE

Yeah. [*Stands up and does a squat and other moves, and speaks in a deep voice.*] I am here. [*While throwing karate punches.*] I am. I am!

[*Interviewers laugh.*]

WADA

Please take a seat.

BRUCE LEE

[*Remains standing and extends right fist.*] This fist is the Truth! You know?

ISONO

The fist is the Truth?

BRUCE LEE

[*While performing some moves.*] Cho, cho! Acho! [*Sits on the chair.*] You know? Ah, this is the Truth.

ISONO

Umm... [*Laughs.*] Could you explain it in words please?

BRUCE LEE

[*Waves right hand to express denial.*]

ISONO

No?

BRUCE LEE

There is no word.

ISONO

There is no word?

BRUCE LEE

The Truth is... empty.

ISONO

Empty?

BRUCE LEE

Hmm. Emptiness is the Truth. Vacancy is very important. Never think anything. Be empty!

ISONO

You said in the film, *Enter the Dragon*, or *Moeyo Doragon*, "Don't think, feel." Is that the same meaning?

BRUCE LEE

Ah, don't fear. Don't think about fear! Oh, yeah, it's a great enemy. Fear!

ISONO

No, no, no, I...

BRUCE LEE

Fear! Fear is the entity of the devil!

ISONO

Sorry, my pronunciation was bad.

BRUCE LEE

Hmm?

ISONO

I said, "Don't think, *feel*."

BRUCE LEE

Ah! Feel!

ISONO

Yes, I said "feel."

BRUCE LEE

You said "feel"?

ISONO

Yes. Sorry, my pronunciation was bad.

BRUCE LEE

I see! I heard *fear*... [*Laughs.*]

Jeet Kune Do is "the world's most beautiful and Strongest martial art"

ISONO

Sorry. You said the Truth is empty and emptiness is the Truth.

BRUCE LEE

Arrrrghhh! [*Stands up and tries to take off jacket, but sits down.*] Oh, [*looks at the mic on left collar*] something bad?

WADA

Yes, there is a microphone.

BRUCE LEE

[*Fans himself.*] Hot. This is Bangkok, right?

ISONO

No.

BRUCE LEE

Bangkok?

ISONO & **WADA**

This is Japan.

BRUCE LEE

Thailand? No?

ISONO

Not Thailand.

WADA

Japan.

BRUCE LEE

Japan? Really? Hot [*fanning himself using the Blu-ray disc case*]. Hot, hotter, hottest. India or Thailand. OK, OK. Your question is?

WADA

You were talking about the spirit of Jeet Kune Do. I would like to ask about the origins of your style. I heard it started with street fighting and then you incorporated...

BRUCE LEE

Good English!

WADA

Thank you, Master Okawa has trained me well.

BRUCE LEE

You are like an American speaking English...

ISONO

Actually, she is a...

WADA

I am American.

BRUCE LEE

You are American!? You're American like me?

WADA

Yes. Yes.

BRUCE LEE
Oh, OK, OK, OK.

WADA
I also lived in San Francisco, so...

BRUCE LEE
Oh, OK, OK. San Francisco English is good English. Yeah, it's OK.

WADA
You incorporated traditional martial arts as well as boxing...

BRUCE LEE
Oh, good pronunciation!

WADA
And fencing...

BRUCE LEE
Oh, beautiful, beautiful! [*Mimics Wada.*] "Martial arts!" Ohoho. Yeah, good!

WADA
And also dancing [*laughs*]. How did you incorporate all these different fields into your martial arts and make it your own style?

BRUCE LEE

Hmm... My father was an actor, this is one thing. And traditional Chinese people, since the 19th century, used to learn kung fu to defend their or our country. We had been intruded by European people. Kung fu means, for example, Japanese *Joi* [meaning "expelling foreigners"]. So, at that time, a man of courage must learn kung fu.

I was a disciple of famous Ip Man and I made a lot of propaganda of kung fu. It had been the pride of the Chinese people, especially the Hong Kong people, and including Chinese Americans. I also succeeded in getting a lot of Japanese fans. In the movie world, I overcame karate martial arts or Judo, so kung fu is worldwide through movies.

In this point only, we can make great victory against white people. We must have something great. We must find some greatness in our traditional culture. This was kung fu.

I rebuilt the kung fu tradition and set up a new type of kung fu. It's Jeet Kune Do. It's the world's most beautiful and strongest martial arts, I think. It's also the strongest one and the most beautiful art of human beings. So, here we can find real strength and real beauty, and here we can achieve the Truth.

What is the Truth? It is the criterion which divides good and evil, or God and devils. You know? From the standpoint of justice, we must destroy the bad people. You must be strong. You know? You know? You know? Happy Science and Jeet Kune Do are almost the same. [*Slowly turning around on the chair as he shows some Jeet Kune Do moves.*] Woo... Poo. Woo.

On the strength, confidence, And justice of martial artists

WADA

You talked about fighting for justice in this world. Would you say that there is a strong relationship between martial arts and religion?

BRUCE LEE

Religion is the teaching of the heart. How to shape up a pure mind and how to get spirituality in your life. This is religion, the way of religion. It's the same.

WADA

I have watched my father practice aikido since I was very young and I always wondered what sort of role the martial artists play in this world. What's their mission?

BRUCE LEE

You mean *roll*?

WADA

Role. Like the martial artists...

BRUCE LEE

Oh, San Francisco roll [he may be referring to California roll, a type of sushi]?

WADA

Like the mission of a martial artist.

BRUCE LEE

Mission? Mission. Mission. OK. Mission. To kill...oh, no. To destroy or knock down evil people. If you're getting stronger and stronger, you can be confident in yourself. At that time, you can be stronger and you can keep justice in your life.

WADA

I watched a documentary about you and you were confident to the point where you seemed a little arrogant. Where does your self-confidence come from? Or, how can we build self-confidence?

BRUCE LEE

That is the way. The true way is nothing. Nothing is vacancy. Vacancy is emptiness. Emptiness is the Truth. Truth is the world. [*Spreads arms up in the air, turns around while sitting on the chair, and gradually speaks in an excited way*.] World is peace. Peace is universe...

ISONO
Please calm...

BRUCE LEE
Universe is, haha, everything! We are in the universe!

3

Taoism and Freedom Believed by Bruce Lee

Asian people can conquer their inferiority complex Toward white people by training

WADA

I would like to ask you about your career in Hollywood.

BRUCE LEE

[*Looks at Wada's face.*] Oh, beautiful. Beautiful. Beautiful. Miss beautiful.

WADA

[*Laughs.*]

BRUCE LEE

Beautiful.

WADA

OK. You were a Hollywood actor and I think you said in the documentary that it was very difficult to get leading roles in movies because of the discrimination or prejudice against Asian people.

BRUCE LEE

Asian people. Discrimination against the Asian people.

WADA

How did you overcome such discrimination to pursue your career?

BRUCE LEE

Martial arts or Japanese bushido. These two ways have one purpose, I mean, the Asian people are smaller than the white people. The white people have much pride in their style, I mean they're tall and rich in muscle. They think that pro boxing is the strongest sport in the world and it's a symbol of the white people's strength.

But in Asia, we have kung fu or bushido. Bushido is a different one, so for example, kung fu. If the person who performs kung fu is a small person, or a small man or woman and a slender person, this kind of small, slender person can defeat a great, big, white champion-like boxer or... as you know, Trump, Mr. Trump, the president. The president is big, but if a small Asian fights with kung fu, Mr. Trump will be knocked down in 60 seconds, I think, one minute or so. It's the starting point of conquering the inferiority complex of the Asian people, I think.

The starting point is how to control your mind and how to make discipline every day, become a confident man or woman and believe in yourself that we have something stronger or we have something more important in us than the spirit of white people or the muscle of white people. So, we are equal in this meaning. Training conquers everything. Not by nature, but by training we can win and we can conquer everything.

Taoism is the Truth of the world

ISONO
You are a great martial artist and great philosopher, I think.

BRUCE LEE
Uh-huh.

ISONO
Because you studied philosophy at university and you studied a wide variety of philosophies from eastern philosophy like Chinese Lao-tzu or Chuang-tzu...

BRUCE LEE
[*Performing some moves as he listens, and reacts to the name Lao-tzu.*] Lao-tzu, ah, Lao-tzu is good.

ISONO
...yes, to western philosophy. What kind of philosophy helped you to succeed?

BRUCE LEE

Taoism is good.

ISONO

Taoism?

BRUCE LEE

Yeah, good. Taoism is good. White is black. Black is white. That is the true explanation... that is the Truth of the world. The world's phenomenon is, something is black while something is white. Black and white make up this world. We cannot live in the white world only or the black world only. We live through these two colored worlds. You must know.

But choose white. If you look at the black world, but go straight, then after that, you can find the white world. In this meaning, "white" doesn't mean the white people. It just means innocent. I mean innocent. Goodness. "Black" means evil or contaminated. I mean that. People sometimes are contaminated by evil thinking, evil tradition, evil culture, or Hitler-like thinking. But we can be white from black. Black sometimes turns out to be white.

Taoism is the Truth. It's the Truth. [*While drawing a big imaginary wave with both hands.*] [see Figure 2.] Our life is like the wave, so sometimes we are in the bottom of the wave and sometimes we are in the upmost point of the wave. Devils usually attack us when we are at the top of the wave. Also, devils attack us when we are in the depths of the wave, but at the same time, angels come to save us. So, the top of the wave and the bottom of the wave, these two points have the truth, in this wavelength, as you know.

Can you understand? [*Turns around on the chair, facing back to the interviewers.*] You cannot, of course... [*Stands up with back facing the interviewers, and throws a right kick.*] Acho! [*Turns around and faces the interviewers, then walks toward Sakai.*] Hmm. You're a fighter. You must fight [*takes a fighting stance*].

SAKAI

[*Laughs.*] No, no, no. Debate, debate.

Figure 2.
The Jeet Kune Do emblem. In the center is the symbol representing the concepts of yin and yang, as in Taoism. The arrows represent the endless interaction between yin and yang and have Bruce Lee's quote, "Using no way as way, having no limitation as limitation."

BRUCE LEE
OK, OK [*sits down on the chair*].

[*Interviewers laugh.*]

"I believe in God"

SAKAI
Could you tell us, Mr. Bruce Lee, have you ever seen an angel?

BRUCE LEE
Oh! Yeah, of course.

SAKAI
Angel?

BRUCE LEE
[*Points to Wada.*] Angel. Here.

SAKAI
Other angels?

BRUCE LEE
[*Points to Sakai.*] Devil.

[*Audience laugh.*]

BRUCE LEE
[*Points to Isono.*] Common man.

SAKAI
What are the criteria to tell between an angel and a devil?

BRUCE LEE
Your heart is black [*audience laugh*]. [*Points to Wada.*] Her heart is white.

SAKAI
Yes, I see.

ISONO
What about me?

BRUCE LEE
You are mediu...

WADA
Medium?

BRUCE LEE
You are medium... [*laughs*] medium rare.

WADA
Gray color?

BRUCE LEE
[*Points to Isono.*] Not well-done. He [Sakai] is well-done.

WADA
It seems that you are a very spiritual person.

BRUCE LEE
Uh-huh. Spiritual.

WADA
Do you believe in God?

BRUCE LEE
Oh, of course, of course! I believe in God and I'm God, too. [*Facing Wada.*] You! Of course, you can find gods or goddesses. We are gods or goddesses. Or, sons or daughters of God or Buddha.

Bruce Lee speaks about harmony and Energy of the universe

ISONO
We think that God has many aspects.

BRUCE LEE
Uh-huh.

ISONO
Or characteristics. So, what kind of aspects of God do you represent?

BRUCE LEE
Aspects?

ISONO
Yes.

BRUCE LEE
Ah. Hmm... Righteousness.

ISONO
Righteousness?

BRUCE LEE
And braveness. Righteousness... braveness... hmm... equality! And freedom! Prosperity! And... love! Peace! Harmony! And receive everything in harmony! Universal harmony! Hmm.

WADA
Did you receive any spiritual inspiration?

BRUCE LEE
[*Preoccupied with his moves, he misses the question.*] Hmm?

WADA
Did you receive any spiritual inspiration from Heaven?

BRUCE LEE
Uh-huh.

WADA
Do you know who it was from?

BRUCE LEE
Lao-tzu. Lao-tzu. Lao-tzu.

ISONO
Lao-tzu? So, Lao-tzu guided you spiritually?

BRUCE LEE
Taoism is my real spiritual parent. I'm the son of Taoism.

ISONO
I think you are also influenced by Buddhism.

BRUCE LEE
Ah, of course, of course. Lao-tzu and Buddha have almost
the same direction of thinking. Buddha taught us, "We have

the chance to become Buddha because we have Buddha-nature in us. So, we need spiritual training." Sometimes we need some kind of physical training, even in Buddhism.

Taoism is a little different, but Taoism also has training. The training is how you feel the energy of the universe. [*Gesturing with both hands.*] Energy of the universe, you gather that kind of energy from the universe within you, and be relaxed. After that, you concentrate [stands up] and attack! [*Throws a punch toward Isono. Isono leans back. Bruce Lee sits back down.*] That is the Truth.

Freedom means to be free from physical bondage

ISONO
Thank you for your precious lesson. I would also like to ask, what is true liberty?

BRUCE LEE
Liberty?

ISONO
Yes. Freedom.

BRUCE LEE
Ah, liberty. Liberty Island.

ISONO
No, not Liberty Island [*laughs*].

BRUCE LEE
Liberty. Hmm. Ah, goddess, the Goddess of Liberty [Statue of Liberty]. I know, I know.

ISONO
Yes.

BRUCE LEE
What's that? What's the problem?

ISONO
No, no.

BRUCE LEE
It's... ah, the Goddess of Liberty. Ah, uh-huh. In that, it's empty. Emptiness. There is emptiness. Yeah, it's true.

ISONO
So, in your teachings, liberty means empty?

BRUCE LEE

No, no.

ISONO

No?

BRUCE LEE

Freedom first.

ISONO

Freedom first?

BRUCE LEE

Freedom. Please set your body free. Set your...ah, your spirit. Please set your spirit free from your bondage, it means your physical condition. This is the true you, yourself.

4

China, Japan, and North Korea as Analyzed by Bruce Lee

Bruce Lee spread the Chinese spirit to the world Through kung fu

WADA

You seem to have a very philosophical side to you. Why did you pursue a career as an actor? You were already a prominent figure in the world of martial arts.

BRUCE LEE

The Chinese people have a 5,000-year history. They are proud of that history. But since the war between China and Europe, in 1840 or so, we have been destroyed by European pragmatism. It's technology regarding war.

But the Chinese people need some symbol like a flag. For example, the American flag or the flag which was held by the Goddess of Freedom, like that. I'm a flag. I am the flag and I am the symbol. I'm the hero of the Chinese people. Not only the Chinese people, but also the American people, the Japanese people, other Asian people or European people loved me and admired me a lot. It's one kind of patriotism dispatched by me, but the Chinese people need some kind of symbol.

So, I am Paul. Paul-of-Christianity-like existence. I mean, I am Paul of kung fu because I spread the beautiful side and the strong side of kung fu. It's a pride of the Chinese spirit, so I spread this kind of Chinese spirit all over the world.

The Chinese people are one-fifth of the world's population, but for a long time, they have been under, how do I say, "the inferiority complex syndrome." So, I am the destroyer of the inferiority complex of the Chinese. I want to be one of the avengers of the U.S.A. As you know, the U.S.A. has several heroes. I want to be one of the heroes of the Americans.

But it was a little difficult, even for me. My wife was a real American citizen, but we, the Chinese, like the Japanese people, were discriminated by white Americans. I sometimes said, "American people say that men are equal and we have freedom and liberty. They say so. But it means equality belongs to white people and freedom and liberty also belong to white people." They despised and disregarded black people and yellow people. When I got married and had a baby, my mother-in-law said, "Oh, I'm going to have a yellow baby." She said so. I was very sorry. I was born in America, but I was physically from China. They had discrimination then.

So, I am the representative of the colored people. Chinese people sometimes dislike the Japanese or sometimes dislike the Korean people, but we must be friends on this point. We must say, "Our soul is equal to the white people." I mean, white, black, and yellow are the same—they all come from God or Buddha.

So, we must show something against the superiority of the white people. In my case, this was kung fu and it got the Hollywood movies involved [see Figure 3 & 4]. It's a very popular way and an effective way for the world. What is the real Chinese spirit and what is the strength of the Chinese people? This was my mission.

[*Speaks to Isono in a joking manner.*] You asked if I'm in Heaven. It's Japanese discrimination against the Chinese. Please apologize to the Chinese people.

Figure 3.
Bruce Lee's name engraved in the Hollywood Walk of Fame. Located on Hollywood Boulevard. Having a name engraved on the Walk of Fame is the greatest honor in Hollywood.

ISONO

No, I don't mean any evil intention toward you.

BRUCE LEE

Really?

ISONO

Yes.

WADA

It's a question we ask many spirits regardless of their race.

BRUCE LEE

Uh-huh.

Figure 4.
A bronze statue stands in Los Angeles, where Bruce Lee once lived.

Movies are a new weapon

ISONO

You succeeded in spreading the spirit of kung fu all over the world through your movies.

BRUCE LEE

Uh-huh.

ISONO

So, I'd like to ask about the mission of movies. What do you think is the mission of movies today?

BRUCE LEE

They are a new weapon for the people. I mean, if we want to know something through newspapers, we must learn how to read or write, or do difficult studying, but when we just watch TV or movies, we can be relaxed and understand or accept something great. It's an easy way and a popular way; spreading of the Truth by movie has ten times the power or one hundred times the power if we compare it to writing a book or something like that, so it's very convenient.

You too, use movies more and more. It's very convenient, and it's easy to be a hero through movies. But the reading population cannot be so many, so it's very difficult.

The Communist Party of China
Will collapse within 10 years

WADA

You talked about equality amongst races, but there are many kung fu movies with strong anti-Japanese sentiment.

BRUCE LEE

Anti-Japanese, OK.

WADA

Also, in China, there is a strong trend to hate Japanese people. What do you think about that?

BRUCE LEE

In my days, China's economic power was very small. Japan was the rising sun at that time, in my days in the 1960s or 70s. At that time, Japan was the sun in the sky and we were just in the light of the moon.

But nowadays, 40 years have passed since then. The Chinese people are getting greater in the economy and have military power now. But they are on the way. I think so. It is said that the Chinese economy is larger than the Japanese one, but in Japan, there are 10 million... no, no, 100 million people. We have more than... I don't know correctly, but ten times as many people as Japan. So, even if the economic size of China is larger than the Japanese one, it does not mean that Japan is inferior to China. Japan has an industrious mind or spirit, and Japan has been the icon of the Asian people for the last 150 years.

Now, the Chinese people think that we can catch up to Japan and overcome Japan this time. They think so, but I think it's a little difficult. Japan is the first country of the Asian countries which defeated European countries, so we must learn something more from Japan. I think so.

China, Korea and Japan, these three must be friends. We must keep the friendship and protect the Asian area from the intrusion of Anglo-Saxon people. China has been intruded many, many times and only Japan could show that power. We must learn from each other and make a tie between us. It's very important, I think. We are not enemies. We must be friends. I think so.

SAKAI

About China, what do you think about the Communist Party of China and Xi Jinping administration? What do you think about it now?

BRUCE LEE

About the communist party, I think China is changing greatly now. I feel a great wave from Hong Kong and the south part of China. China is a country of capitalism now in reality, but they have an illusion that they belong to communism. It's not true. They are living in capitalism.

Japan is now going from capitalism to socialism. I think so. Japan is just seeking equality, not the growth of the economy, but equality in the result of economic activity.

But look at China. They are seeking wealth and they are working for their own wealth ardently. Quite different. China is just in the Meiji period of Japan. Changing, changing, changing, changing.

So, the Communist Party of China will collapse in the near future, I mean within 10 years because the Chinese economic size is a very huge one. It's competing with the American economy. It means China will change into a capitalist country, for the Chinese people are living to earn money. As you know, they don't have much intention in spiritual development, but I think, as you know, people need food and livelihood, I mean food, house and clothes. After that, people can seek a pure spiritual living.

China is just moving, so don't think too rapidly about that. They will become a Japanese-like country and an American-like country in these 10 or 20 years. And, the beginning of capitalism, I mean the culture which allows you to get money from huge reputation, started from Bruce Lee. I'm the starting point of capitalism of the Hong Kong Chinese [*laughs*].

ISONO

OK. Then, I'd like to ask about the current situation in China and Hong Kong, since we are greatly concerned about that. The Chinese government suppresses the liberty of the Chinese people and there is the "one country, two systems" policy in Hong Kong, but the Chinese government invaded and deprived the people of Hong Kong of their liberty. So, what do you think about the current situation?

BRUCE LEE

Then, how about Duterte of the Philippines? He killed a lot because of his policy on drugs.

ISONO

Hmm.

BRUCE LEE

More than China. He killed a lot of people. Maybe seven hundred or eight hundred thousand? I'm not sure, but maybe almost one million people were killed by President Duterte because of drug dealers or drug users*. It's more than the Chinese government, I think. America usually attacks Chinese policies because of the lack of humanity.

---

* In reality, it is reported that several thousand people were killed during his search for drug users, and a million turned themselves in out of fear of being killed.

It means the government puts pressure on weaker people or poor people. But now, even America cannot say like that because America itself has very much difference between the richest people and the poorest people. So, America is almost the same as China.

We must think about that seriously, of course. But firstly, there are the people who are talented in something, for example, kung fu, being beautiful, writing books, teaching something or showing something, and getting great money. After that, people learn from them and follow them. And after that, social welfare must remake the country politics. I think so.

As you said, China has a lot of problems, but 30 or 40 years ago, I mean in my age, in my period, almost all Chinese people were very poor at that time. But now, 20 or 30 percent of the Chinese people are richer than before. It's getting better and better, so just give them the time.

And, a lot of Chinese people have been going abroad, especially to the United States, studying in the United States universities or getting an MBA from a famous university in the U.S.A., and returning back to China. Now, they are still not so old; they are 20, 30, or 40 years old. But 10 or 20 years in the future, they will get real influence on politics, economy, and education. Then, China will change greatly. I hope so.

ISONO

Does that mean you support the current Chinese government's policies?

BRUCE LEE

No. I don't support. I just said I'm the first one.

There will be another hero after Liu Xiaobo

ISONO

So next, the future generations of China will change the government or regime?

BRUCE LEE

The Chinese people need a hero, and I am the hero. One part of Chinese culture is kung fu, but there are other parts of the culture. Other heroes will appear after me and follow me. They will continue to fight against all systems and they will finally win. I think so.

SAKAI

Do you know who Liu Xiaobo is?

BRUCE LEE

I know.

SAKAI

He is a hero, I think.

BRUCE LEE

Uh-huh.

SAKAI

What do you think about him?

BRUCE LEE

He's OK, but he is not Bruce Lee. He is before Bruce Lee. After his death, there will appear a Bruce Lee, a political performer, and the political reformer will succeed in the real revolution for freedom. I think so.

China selected economy first and politics later. It was made in the 1980s or 1990s, around then. So, economy first and politics will follow, I think. Xi Jinping is not so good at developing the economy, so he is just attacking the politicians who get a lot of money by dint of their political power. He says, "We'll kill tigers and flies, both.*" It means a man who has great power and a man who has small power, both who commit crimes will be banished from the Chinese central political position. He insists so. It's an old style. I know it's an old style. It's maybe a style

---

* A slogan used by Xi Jinping in his anti-corruption campaign. "Tigers" means high-ranking officials while "flies" means petty civil servants. Simply put, corruptions will be exposed regardless of position.

used before the Meiji Restoration, I mean the Edo period, I think. But China is, at this time, at that level, but after that, they will change. I think so.

North Korea should ask Japan to rescue them

WADA

I would like to ask about North Korea.

BRUCE LEE

North Korea!? Ah...

WADA

Now, Mr. Trump has been threatening North Korea and the relationship between the United States, China and Japan is very unstable. How can we resolve this or what do you think about this situation?

BRUCE LEE

Hmm, very complicated because the emotion of North Korean people and South Korean people is very confusing, I mean they are educated to hate Japanese people historically. But they are also taught, "America is the new intruder, so be careful."

Especially, North Korea has no friends. The only friend is China, but China is greatly changing now. China's trading amount is... the China-American trade amount is number one. So, in thinking from the standpoint of trading profit, even Xi Jinping will finally give up on North Korea.

They will choose America because America, the United States, will make China a wealthier country, but North Korea just says, "Give us money. Give us goods. Give us food." It's pity indeed, but as one of the largest countries of the world, the Chinese top leader, even if it's Xi Jinping or another person, will choose what is big and what is small. They can understand the reason why.

So, North Korea should change their attitude. They don't believe that they will be abandoned by Beijing in the near future, but in reality, Beijing will give up North Korea because they are bad in their behavior.

Also, they are educated to look down upon Japan. But Japan is a strong country and a very intelligent country. All over, the Japanese people can read and learn a lot of knowledge. People who can read, speak, and hear Japanese language... The Japanese language guarantees the people to become intelligent as the world's top level.

Even the Chinese people and the Korean people are proud that they are good at speaking English. They are proud of that, but the Japanese people learn from Japanese books, Japanese news, or Japanese wisdom, how to live and what their future is. The Japanese people are quite contrary to the European people and other Asian people. Japan is another civilization, I think. This is very strong and a very excellent one.

So, North Korea will lose two points. I mean, first, the support of Beijing. And, they must learn from Japan a lot, but they dislike it and they will lose the chance to save themselves. Japan can save North Korea, of course, but their behavior is very bad. So, Japan doesn't work.

The last question is, when will the United States attack North Korea, or will they not attack? Japan is just observer-like people, but North Korea must ask for some rescue from Japan. I think so.

ISONO
Thank you.

5

Bruce Lee Reveals His Past Life, The Truth of His Death, And the Mission of His Soul

"I was a dragon in every time"

SAKAI

Another question. I would like to know about your past life. Do you know what your past life is?

BRUCE LEE

Past life, hmm... [*Picks up and looks at the Enter the Dragon Blu-ray disc case*] Dragon [*smiles toward the camera as he shows the case*].

SAKAI

Dragon? Not human, but a dragon?

BRUCE LEE

Dragon.

SAKAI

You are a dragon?

BRUCE LEE

Dragon. A dragon [*laughs*].

ISONO

Do you mean in this world or in another world?

BRUCE LEE

Huh? In every time... I was a dragon, I mean a hero.

ISONO

Have you always been a hero?

BRUCE LEE

Yeah.

ISONO

Do you have any memory living in China or other countries?

BRUCE LEE

Hmm... There have been a lot of dragons in China, Japan, and other Asian countries and of course, in the ancient time, in the Middle East, Africa, and Europe. I have been a dragon.

Sometimes a warrior, of course, of course. Sometimes I was a warrior. And sometimes... [*Thinks for a moment.*] Umm... warrior [*laughs*]. Oh, yeah [*laughs*].

ISONO

So, you are always a warrior and fighting against evil.

BRUCE LEE

Yeah.

SAKAI

What about in Japan?

BRUCE LEE

Ah, hmm... Maybe a ninja, like that [*laughs*]. *Iga* ninja, like that [*laughs*].

SAKAI

I heard you were a shogun in the Muromachi *bakufu*.

BRUCE LEE

Ah, shogun?

SAKAI

Shogun.

BRUCE LEE

You say that, but I've heard that in your book, you wrote that Lee Teng-hui of Taiwan was a shogun of Ashikaga bakufu.* So, I must stop my saying. Warrior, just a warrior. It's an easy way, but it's OK.

SAKAI

But who do you think is the reincarnation of Ashikaga Yoshiteru?

BRUCE LEE

I don't know, I don't know, I don't know. I was usually a warrior. Maybe I was strong, as strong as Ashikaga Yoshiteru's teacher.

SAKAI

Tsukahara Bokuden[†]?

BRUCE LEE

Tsukahara Bokuden, ah... I don't know exactly, but I must have been some kind of grand master. You have a lot of grand masters in bushido, so please choose a suitable one.

SAKAI

Suitable one, OK.

---

[*] In his spiritual interview, the guardian spirit of Lee Teng-hui said that he was Yoshiteru Ashikaga (1536 - 1565), the 13th Shogun of the Muromachi government of Japan, in his past life. See *Japan! Regain Your Samurai Spirit: A Message from the Guardian Spirit of Lee Teng-hui, Former President of the Republic of China* (New York: IRH Press, 2014).

[†] A master swordsman in the late Muromachi period (16th century) of Japan. He is believed to have been the instructor of sword fighting for Yoshiteru Ashikaga.

ISONO

I also heard you had a memory of being born as Lin Chong*.

BRUCE LEE

Oh, it's a fiction.

ISONO

Fiction?

BRUCE LEE

It's fiction writing, so...

ISONO

So, it was not true?

BRUCE LEE

But in some meaning, it's true. I'm good at using a spear, you know? Long, sword-like spear. [*Acts as if using a spear.*] Shakespeare†, you know? Yeah. [*Speaks to Sakai.*] As you did [in your past life]. You are a master.

SAKAI

No, no.

---

* A fictional character in *Water Margin*, a Chinese novel printed in the Ming dynasty in the 16th century. An expert spearman.

† The name Shakespeare comes from "shake" and "spear."

BRUCE LEE

You are a master of spears.

The spiritual truth of his early death

WADA

I think you had a very big mission here on earth, but you died very young. Were you able to accomplish everything you were supposed to?

BRUCE LEE

No.

WADA

How did you die?

BRUCE LEE

[*Sighs deeply.*] I had an accident in my back in my twenties and I did too much in my movies, so it must have been the direct reason of my young death.

Another reason is, I had enemies which could not be seen through my human eyes. I sometimes said devils. Devils were attacking me. Devils don't like heroes. A hero is sometimes the assistant of God, so heroes are targeted by devils. It's like Ryoma Sakamoto, who died too young.

He died too young, the same age as when I died. We are on the verge of losing our lives, every year, every age, and every period.

We have a mind of *fushaku shimmyo*,* of course, because we are the destroyers of the old age. So, the people who protect the old age sometimes kill us and even the devils will give powers to them. I was a hero from Heaven, but some devils want to destroy the Chinese new legacy, I mean the hope of the Chinese people.

It is the real meaning of my young death. So, I died too young. [*Points to Wada.*] If you want to get married in the near future [*smiles while doing the eyebrow flash*], I will be waiting.

WADA
[*Laughs.*]

Bruce Lee's mission as a destroyer of the old age

SAKAI
Now, you said "from Heaven."

BRUCE LEE
Yeah, of course, of course, hero of God.

---

* A Buddhist term meaning, "devoting one's life."

SAKAI

Where do you live? Where are you? Now, another world, in Heaven?

BRUCE LEE

My living room is very small, so I don't know correctly. Your living room is very huge. But I'm a friend of Ryoma Sakamoto*, you know? That's enough explanation for you.

SAKAI

Same dimension†?

BRUCE LEE

Ah, no, no. Sometimes, we are friends.

SAKAI

Friends? Do you know other friends?

---

* Ryoma Sakamoto (1835 - 1867) was a revolutionary from a period before the Meiji Restoration who was from Tosa clan.

† According to Happy Science, the Spirit World is divided into dimensions from four to nine in accordance to the levels of enlightenment. The lower part of the fourth dimension is Hell, the dimensions above the fifth are Heaven. Those with good hearts reside in the fifth dimension, leaders and experts in the sixth, angels in the seventh, great angels in the eight, and saviors in the ninth dimension. Refer to *The Laws of the Sun* (New York: IRH Press, 2013) and *The Nine Dimensions* (New York: IRH Press, 2012).

BRUCE LEE

[*Points to Ryoma as if he is behind Bruce Lee.*] A destroyer of the Edo period.

SAKAI

A destroyer, yeah, yeah.

BRUCE LEE

I'm a destroyer of the Chinese age of slavery.

SAKAI

Ah, OK.

ISONO

So, you destroy the old age and create a new one.

BRUCE LEE

Yeah, and I want to be a bridge between China and Japan, China and Hong Kong, and Hong Kong and the U.S.A., Europe, and other Asian countries. I hope so. I hope so.

ISONO

This is the last question from me. Could you give a message to the people of China and the world?

BRUCE LEE

Learn kung fu and study Happy Science.

ISONO

That's all?

BRUCE LEE

That's all.

ISONO

OK, thank you very much.

BRUCE LEE

Is it OK? [*Takes a Jeet Kune Do stance.*] Do you need my new action? [*While moving both hands.*] Acho, acho! Ohh! Voice is a power! You know? You must invent a new voice. Mr. Okawa should stand at Tokyo Dome and should say, "[*Takes a stance.*] Acho!! [*As if pointing at the enemy.*] Chinese, I will punish you! Change your mind. Acho!" He should say so.

SAKAI

What is the meaning of "acho"?

BRUCE LEE

Acho means the Voice of God. Uh-huh.

ISONO
What does it mean?

BRUCE LEE
Umm, "I will destroy you."

ISONO
"Destroy, punish you"?

BRUCE LEE
"Punish you."

ISONO
I see.

SAKAI
Thank you.

BRUCE LEE
Is it OK?

SAKAI
It's OK.

BRUCE LEE
Is it enough? You enjoyed?

ISONO

Very much.

BRUCE LEE

Enjoyed? OK. You are a good man.

INTERVIEWERS

Yes, thank you very much.

BRUCE LEE

Bye-bye.

After the spiritual interview

RYUHO OKAWA

[*Claps three times.*] Ah, funny guy. Bruce Lee was "the Bruce Lee." Not less than Bruce Lee, not more than Bruce Lee.

He was a hero, but not the Chinese hero only. He was a citizen of the United States and he has a lot of fans in Japan. He has influence, a lot of influence all over the world. I think so. I hope so.

Thank you, Bruce Lee.

INTERVIEWERS

Thank you very much, Master Okawa.

ABOUT THE AUTHOR

Founder and CEO of Happy Science Group.

Ryuho Okawa was born on July 7th 1956, in Tokushima, Japan. After graduating from the University of Tokyo with a law degree, he joined a Tokyo-based trading house. While working at its New York headquarters, he studied international finance at the Graduate Center of the City University of New York. In 1981, he attained Great Enlightenment and became aware that he is El Cantare with a mission to bring salvation to all humankind.

In 1986, he established Happy Science. It now has members in over 165 countries across the world, with more than 700 branches and temples as well as 10,000 missionary houses around the world.

He has given over 3,400 lectures (of which more than 150 are in English) and published over 3,000 books (of which more than 600 are Spiritual Interview Series), and many are translated into 40 languages. Along with *The Laws of the Sun* and *The Laws Of Messiah*, many of the books have become best sellers or million sellers. To date, Happy Science has produced 25 movies. The original story and original concept were given by the Executive Producer Ryuho Okawa. He has also composed music and written lyrics of over 450 pieces.

Moreover, he is the Founder of Happy Science University and Happy Science Academy (Junior and Senior High School), Founder and President of the Happiness Realization Party, Founder and Honorary Headmaster of Happy Science Institute of Government and Management, Founder of IRH Press Co., Ltd., and the Chairperson of NEW STAR PRODUCTION Co., Ltd. and ARI Production Co., Ltd.

WHAT IS EL CANTARE?

El Cantare means "the Light of the Earth," and is the Supreme God of the Earth who has been guiding humankind since the beginning of Genesis. He is whom Jesus called Father and Muhammad called Allah, and is *Ame-no-Mioya-Gami*, Japanese Father God. Different parts of El Cantare's core consciousness have descended to Earth in the past, once as Alpha and another as Elohim. His branch spirits, such as Shakyamuni Buddha and Hermes, have descended to Earth many times and helped to flourish many civilizations. To unite various religions and to integrate various fields of study in order to build a new civilization on Earth, a part of the core consciousness has descended to Earth as Master Ryuho Okawa.

Alpha is a part of the core consciousness of El Cantare who descended to Earth around 330 million years ago. Alpha preached Earth's Truths to harmonize and unify Earth-born humans and space people who came from other planets.

Elohim is a part of El Cantare's core consciousness who descended to Earth around 150 million years ago. He gave wisdom, mainly on the differences of light and darkness, good and evil.

Ame-no-Mioya-Gami (Japanese Father God) is the Creator God and the Father God who appears in the ancient literature, *Hotsuma Tsutae*. It is believed that He descended on the foothills of Mt. Fuji about 30,000 years ago and built the Fuji dynasty, which is the root of the Japanese civilization. With justice as the central pillar, Ame-no-Mioya-Gami's teachings spread to ancient civilizations of other countries in the world.

Shakyamuni Buddha was born as a prince into the Shakya Clan in India around 2,600 years ago. When he was 29 years old, he renounced the world and sought enlightenment. He later attained Great Enlightenment and founded Buddhism.

Hermes is one of the 12 Olympian gods in Greek mythology, but the spiritual Truth is that he taught the teachings of love and progress around 4,300 years ago that became the origin of the current Western civilization. He is a hero that truly existed.

Ophealis was born in Greece around 6,500 years ago and was the leader who took an expedition to as far as Egypt. He is the God of miracles, prosperity, and arts, and is known as Osiris in the Egyptian mythology.

Rient Arl Croud was born as a king of the ancient Incan Empire around 7,000 years ago and taught about the mysteries of the mind. In the heavenly world, he is responsible for the interactions that take place between various planets.

Thoth was an almighty leader who built the golden age of the Atlantic civilization around 12,000 years ago. In the Egyptian mythology, he is known as god Thoth.

Ra Mu was a leader who built the golden age of the civilization of Mu around 17,000 years ago. As a religious leader and a politician, he ruled by uniting religion and politics.

WHAT IS A SPIRITUAL MESSAGE?

We are all spiritual beings living on this earth. The following is the mechanism behind Master Ryuho Okawa's spiritual messages.

1 You are a spirit

People are born into this world to gain wisdom through various experiences and return to the other world when their lives end. We are all spirits and repeat this cycle in order to refine our souls.

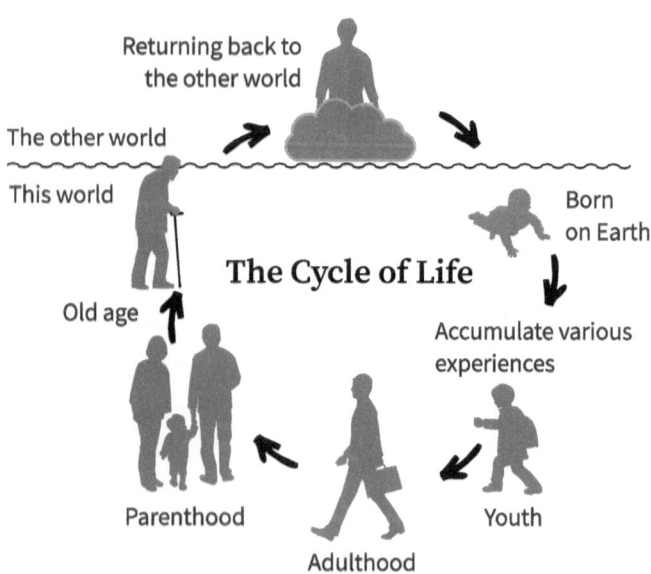

Returning back to the other world

The other world

This world

Old age

The Cycle of Life

Born on Earth

Accumulate various experiences

Parenthood

Adulthood

Youth

2 You have a guardian spirit

Guardian spirits are those who protect the people who are living on this earth. Each of us has a guardian spirit that watches over us and guides us from the other world. They were us in our past life, and are identical in how we think.

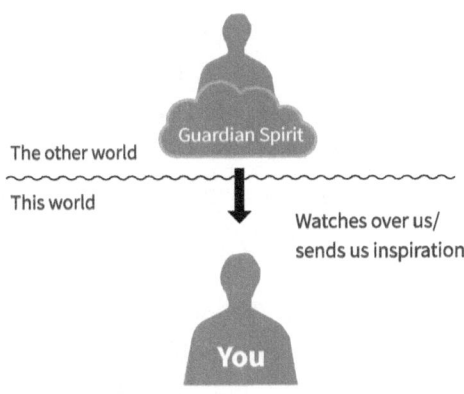

3 How spiritual messages work

Master Ryuho Okawa, through his enlightenment, is capable of summoning any spirit from anywhere in the world, including the spirit world.

Master Okawa's way of receiving spiritual messages is fundamentally different from that of other psychic mediums who undergo trances and are thereby completely taken over by the spirits they are channeling.

Master Okawa's attainment of a high level of enlightenment enables him to retain full control of his consciousness and body throughout the duration of the spiritual message. To allow the spirits to express their own thoughts and personalities freely, however, Master Okawa usually softens the dominancy of his consciousness. This way, he is able to keep his own philosophies out of the way and ensure that the spiritual messages are pure expressions of the spirits he is channeling.

Since guardian spirits think at the same subconscious level as the person living on earth, Master Okawa can summon the spirit and find out what the person on earth is actually thinking. If the person has already returned to the other world, the spirit can give messages to the people living on earth through Master Okawa.

Since 2009, many spiritual messages have been openly recorded by Master Okawa and published. Spiritual messages from the guardian spirits of people living today such as Donald Trump, former Japanese Prime Minister Shinzo Abe and Chinese President Xi Jinping, as well as spiritual messages sent from the spirit world by Jesus Christ, Muhammad, Thomas Edison, Mother Teresa, Steve Jobs and Nelson Mandela are just a tiny pack of spiritual messages that were published so far.

Domestically, in Japan, these spiritual messages are being read by a wide range of politicians and mass media, and the high-level contents of these books are delivering an impact even more on politics, news and public opinion. In recent years, there have been spiritual messages recorded in English, and

English translations are being done on the spiritual messages given in Japanese. These have been published overseas, one after another, and have started to shake the world.

1. The guardian spirit / spirit in the other world...

2. Goes inside Master Okawa in this world

3. Master Okawa speaks the words of the guardian spirit / spirit

For more about spiritual messages and a complete list of books in the Spiritual Interview Series, visit okawabooks.com

ABOUT HAPPY SCIENCE

Happy Science is a global movement that empowers individuals to find purpose and spiritual happiness and to share that happiness with their families, societies, and the world. With more than 12 million members around the world, Happy Science aims to increase awareness of spiritual truths and expand our capacity for love, compassion, and joy so that together we can create the kind of world we all wish to live in.

Activities at Happy Science are based on the Principle of Happiness (Love, Wisdom, Self-Reflection, and Progress). This principle embraces worldwide philosophies and beliefs, transcending boundaries of culture and religions.

Love teaches us to give ourselves freely without expecting anything in return; it encompasses giving, nurturing, and forgiving.

Wisdom leads us to the insights of spiritual truths, and opens us to the true meaning of life and the will of God (the universe, the highest power, Buddha).

Self-Reflection brings a mindful, nonjudgmental lens to our thoughts and actions to help us find our truest selves—the essence of our souls—and deepen our connection to the highest power. It helps us attain a clean and peaceful mind and leads us to the right life path.

Progress emphasizes the positive, dynamic aspects of our spiritual growth—actions we can take to manifest and spread happiness around the world. It's a path that not only expands our soul growth, but also furthers the collective potential of the world we live in.

PROGRAMS AND EVENTS

The doors of Happy Science are open to all. We offer a variety of programs and events, including self-exploration and self-growth programs, spiritual seminars, meditation and contemplation sessions, study groups, and book events.

Our programs are designed to:
* Deepen your understanding of your purpose and meaning in life
* Improve your relationships and increase your capacity to love unconditionally
* Attain peace of mind, decrease anxiety and stress, and feel positive
* Gain deeper insights and a broader perspective on the world
* Learn how to overcome life's challenges
  ... and much more.

For more information, visit <u>happy-science.org</u>.

OUR ACTIVITIES

Happy Science does other various activities to provide support for those in need.

◆ **You Are An Angel! General Incorporated Association**

Happy Science has a volunteer network in Japan that encourages and supports children with disabilities as well as their parents and guardians.

◆ **Never Mind School for Truancy**

At 'Never Mind,' we support students who find it very challenging to attend schools in Japan. We also nurture their self-help spirit and power to rebound against obstacles in life based on Master Okawa's teachings and faith.

◆ **"Prevention Against Suicide" Campaign since 2003**

A nationwide campaign to reduce suicides; over 20,000 people commit suicide every year in Japan. "The Suicide Prevention Website-Words of Truth for You-" presents spiritual prescriptions for worries such as depression, lost love, extramarital affairs, bullying and work-related problems, thereby saving many lives.

◆ **Support for Anti-bullying Campaigns**

Happy Science provides support for a group of parents and guardians, Network to Protect Children from Bullying, a general incorporated foundation launched in Japan to end bullying, including those that can even be called a criminal offense. So far, the network received more than 5,000 cases and resolved 90% of them.

- **The Golden Age Scholarship**

  This scholarship is granted to students who can contribute greatly and bring a hopeful future to the world.

- **Success No.1**
  Buddha's Truth Afterschool Academy

  Happy Science has over 180 classrooms throughout Japan and in several cities around the world that focus on afterschool education for children. The education focuses on faith and morals in addition to supporting children's school studies.

- **Angel Plan V**

  For children under the age of kindergarten, Happy Science holds classes for nurturing healthy, positive, and creative boys and girls.

- **Future Stars Training Department**

  The Future Stars Training Department was founded within the Happy Science Media Division with the goal of nurturing talented individuals to become successful in the performing arts and entertainment industry.

- **NEW STAR PRODUCTION Co., Ltd.**
  ARI Production Co., Ltd.

  We have companies to nurture actors and actresses, artists, and vocalists. They are also involved in film production.

CONTACT INFORMATION

Happy Science is a worldwide organization with branches and temples around the globe. For a comprehensive list, visit the worldwide directory at *happy-science.org*. The following are some of the many Happy Science locations:

UNITED STATES AND CANADA

New York
79 Franklin St., New York, NY 10013, USA
Phone: 1-212-343-7972
Fax: 1-212-343-7973
Email: ny@happy-science.org
Website: happyscience-usa.org

New Jersey
66 Hudson St., #2R, Hoboken, NJ 07030, USA
Phone: 1-201-313-0127
Email: nj@happy-science.org
Website: happyscience-usa.org

Chicago
2300 Barrington Rd., Suite #400,
Hoffman Estates, IL 60169, USA
Phone: 1-630-937-3077
Email: chicago@happy-science.org
Website: happyscience-usa.org

Florida
5208 8th St., Zephyrhills, FL 33542, USA
Phone: 1-813-715-0000
Fax: 1-813-715-0010
Email: florida@happy-science.org
Website: happyscience-usa.org

Atlanta
1874 Piedmont Ave., NE Suite 360-C
Atlanta, GA 30324, USA
Phone: 1-404-892-7770
Email: atlanta@happy-science.org
Website: happyscience-usa.org

San Francisco
525 Clinton St.
Redwood City, CA 94062, USA
Phone & Fax: 1-650-363-2777
Email: sf@happy-science.org
Website: happyscience-usa.org

Los Angeles
1590 E. Del Mar Blvd., Pasadena, CA 91106, USA
Phone: 1-626-395-7775
Fax: 1-626-395-7776
Email: la@happy-science.org
Website: happyscience-usa.org

Orange County
16541 Gothard St. Suite 104
Huntington Beach, CA 92647
Phone: 1-714-659-1501
Email: oc@happy-science.org
Website: happyscience-usa.org

San Diego
7841 Balboa Ave. Suite #202
San Diego, CA 92111, USA
Phone: 1-626-395-7775
Fax: 1-626-395-7776
E-mail: sandiego@happy-science.org
Website: happyscience-usa.org

Hawaii
Phone: 1-808-591-9772
Fax: 1-808-591-9776
Email: hi@happy-science.org
Website: happyscience-usa.org

Kauai
3343 Kanakolu Street, Suite 5
Lihue, HI 96766, USA
Phone: 1-808-822-7007
Fax: 1-808-822-6007
Email: kauai-hi@happy-science.org
Website: happyscience-usa.org

Toronto

845 The Queensway
Etobicoke, ON M8Z 1N6, Canada
Phone: 1-416-901-3747
Email: toronto@happy-science.org
Website: happy-science.ca

Vancouver

#201-2607 East 49th Avenue,
Vancouver, BC, V5S 1J9, Canada
Phone: 1-604-437-7735
Fax: 1-604-437-7764
Email: vancouver@happy-science.org
Website: happy-science.ca

INTERNATIONAL

Tokyo

1-6-7 Togoshi, Shinagawa,
Tokyo, 142-0041, Japan
Phone: 81-3-6384-5770
Fax: 81-3-6384-5776
Email: tokyo@happy-science.org
Website: happy-science.org

Seoul

74, Sadang-ro 27-gil,
Dongjak-gu, Seoul, Korea
Phone: 82-2-3478-8777
Fax: 82-2-3478-9777
Email: korea@happy-science.org
Website: happyscience-korea.org

London

3 Margaret St.
London, W1W 8RE United Kingdom
Phone: 44-20-7323-9255
Fax: 44-20-7323-9344
Email: eu@happy-science.org
Website: www.happyscience-uk.org

Taipei

No. 89, Lane 155, Dunhua N. Road,
Songshan District, Taipei City 105, Taiwan
Phone: 886-2-2719-9377
Fax: 886-2-2719-5570
Email: taiwan@happy-science.org
Website: happyscience-tw.org

Sydney

516 Pacific Highway, Lane Cove North,
2066 NSW, Australia
Phone: 61-2-9411-2877
Fax: 61-2-9411-2822
Email: sydney@happy-science.org

Kuala Lumpur

No 22A, Block 2, Jalil Link Jalan Jalil
Jaya 2, Bukit Jalil 57000,
Kuala Lumpur, Malaysia
Phone: 60-3-8998-7877
Fax: 60-3-8998-7977
Email: malaysia@happy-science.org
Website: happyscience.org.my

Sao Paulo

Rua. Domingos de Morais 1154,
Vila Mariana, Sao Paulo SP
CEP 04010-100, Brazil
Phone: 55-11-5088-3800
Email: sp@happy-science.org
Website: happyscience.com.br

Kathmandu

Kathmandu Metropolitan City,
Ward No. 15, Ring Road, Kimdol,
Sitapaila Kathmandu, Nepal
Phone: 977-1-427-2931
Email: nepal@happy-science.org

Jundiai

Rua Congo, 447, Jd. Bonfiglioli
Jundiai-CEP, 13207-340, Brazil
Phone: 55-11-4587-5952
Email: jundiai@happy-science.org

Kampala

Plot 877 Rubaga Road, Kampala
P.O. Box 34130 Kampala, UGANDA
Phone: 256-79-4682-121
Email: uganda@happy-science.org

ABOUT HAPPINESS REALIZATION PARTY

The Happiness Realization Party (HRP) was founded in May 2009 by Master Ryuho Okawa as part of the Happy Science Group. HRP strives to improve the Japanese society, based on three basic political principles of "freedom, democracy, and faith," and let Japan promote individual and public happiness from Asia to the world as a leader nation.

1) Diplomacy and Security: Protecting Freedom, Democracy, and Faith of Japan and the World from China's Totalitarianism

Japan's current defense system is insufficient against China's expanding hegemony and the threat of North Korea's nuclear missiles. Japan, as the leader of Asia, must strengthen its defense power and promote strategic diplomacy together with the nations which share the values of freedom, democracy, and faith. Further, HRP aims to realize world peace under the leadership of Japan, the nation with the spirit of religious tolerance.

2) Economy: Early economic recovery through utilizing the "wisdom of the private sector"

Economy has been damaged severely by the novel coronavirus originated in China. Many companies have been forced into bankruptcy or out of business. What is needed for economic recovery now is not subsidies and regulations by the government, but policies which can utilize the "wisdom of the private sector."

For more information, visit en.hr-party.jp

HAPPY SCIENCE ACADEMY JUNIOR AND SENIOR HIGH SCHOOL

Happy Science Academy Junior and Senior High School is a boarding school founded with the goal of educating the future leaders of the world who can have a big vision, persevere, and take on new challenges.

Currently, there are two campuses in Japan; the Nasu Main Campus in Tochigi Prefecture, founded in 2010, and the Kansai Campus in Shiga Prefecture, founded in 2013.

Nasu Main Campus

Kansai Campus

HAPPY SCIENCE UNIVERSITY

THE FOUNDING SPIRIT AND THE GOAL OF EDUCATION

Based on the founding philosophy of the university, "Exploration of happiness and the creation of a new civilization," education, research and studies will be provided to help students acquire deep understanding grounded in religious belief and advanced expertise with the objectives of producing "great talents of virtue" who can contribute in a broad-ranging way to serve Japan and the international society.

FACULTIES

Faculty of human happiness

Students in this faculty will pursue liberal arts from various perspectives with a multidisciplinary approach, explore and envision an ideal state of human beings and society.

Faculty of successful management

This faculty aims to realize successful management that helps organizations to create value and wealth for society and to contribute to the happiness and the development of management and employees as well as society as a whole.

Faculty of future creation

Students in this faculty study subjects such as political science, journalism, performing arts and artistic expression, and explore and present new political and cultural models based on truth, goodness and beauty.

Faculty of future industry

This faculty aims to nurture engineers who can resolve various issues facing modern civilization from a technological standpoint and contribute to the creation of new industries of the future.

ABOUT HS PRESS

HS Press is an imprint of IRH Press Co., Ltd. IRH Press Co., Ltd., based in Tokyo, was founded in 1987 as a publishing division of Happy Science. IRH Press publishes religious and spiritual books, journals, magazines and also operates broadcast and film production enterprises. For more information, visit *okawabooks.com*.

Follow us on:

f Facebook: Okawa Books   Instagram: OkawaBooks
▶ Youtube: Okawa Books   **🐦** Twitter: Okawa Books
P Pinterest: Okawa Books   **g** Goodreads: Ryuho Okawa

--- **NEWSLETTER** ---

To receive book related news, promotions and events, please subscribe to our newsletter below.

∞ eepurl.com/bsMeJj

 --- **AUDIO / VISUAL MEDIA** ---

YOUTUBE   PODCAST

Introduction of Ryuho Okawa's titles; topics ranging from self-help, current affairs, spirituality, religion, and the universe.

BOOKS BY RYUHO OKAWA

THE LAWS OF MISSION

ESSENTIAL TRUTHS FOR SPIRITUAL AWAKENING IN A SECULAR AGE

In this day and age of advanced scientific and information technology, we are often deluded by a false sense that we know everything. But in fact, many people cannot even answer simple but fundamental questions about life, such as "what's the purpose of our life" and "what happens after death."

In this book, Ryuho Okawa offers integral spiritual truths that bring about spiritual awakening within each of us. This book helps us find the purpose and meaning of our life and make the right decisions so that we can walk on the path to happiness.

For a complete list of books, visit okawabooks.com

THE LAWS OF JUSTICE
HOW WE CAN SOLVE
WORLD CONFLICTS & BRING PEACE

How can we solve conflicts in this world? Why is it that we continue to live in a world of turmoil, when we all wish to live in a world of peace and harmony?

In recent years, we've faced issues that jeopardize international peace and security, including the rise of ISIS, Syrian civil war and refugee crisis, break-off of diplomatic relations between Saudi Arabia and Iran, Russia's annexation of Crimea, China's military expansion, and North Korea's nuclear development.

This book shows what global justice is from a comprehensive perspective of the Supreme God. Becoming aware of this view will let us embrace differences in beliefs, recognize other people's divine nature, and love and forgive one another. It will also become the key to solving the issues we face, whether they're religious, political, societal, economic, or academic, and help the world become a better and safer world for all of us living today.

For a complete list of books, visit okawabooks.com

THE TRUMP SECRET
Seeing Through the Past, Present, and Future of the New American President

Donald Trump's victory in the 2016 presidential election surprised almost all major vote forecasters who predicted Hillary Clinton's victory. But 10 months earlier, in January 2016, Ryuho Okawa, Global Visionary, a renowned spiritual leader, and international best-selling author, had already foreseen Trump's victory. This book contains a series of lectures and interviews that unveil the secrets to Trump's victory and makes predictions of what will happen under his presidency. This book predicts the coming of a new America that will go through a great transformation from the "red and blue states" to the United States.

Contents

Chapter 1: On Victory of Mr. Donald Trump

Chapter 2: Freedom, Justice, and Happiness

Chapter 3: Spiritual Interview with George Washington

Chapter 4: The Trump Card in the United States

For a complete list of books, visit okawabooks.com

THE LAWS OF THE SUN

ONE SOURCE, ONE PLANET, ONE PEOPLE

Imagine if you could ask God why He created this world and what spiritual laws He used to shape us—and everything around us. If we could understand His designs and intentions, we could discover what our goals in life should be and whether our actions move us closer to those goals or farther away.

THE GOLDEN LAWS

HISTORY THROUGH THE EYES OF THE ETERNAL BUDDHA

The Golden Laws reveals how Buddha's Plan has been unfolding on earth, and outlines five thousand years of the secret history of humankind. Once we understand the true course of history, we cannot help but become aware of the significance of our spiritual mission in the present age.

THE NINE DIMENSIONS

UNVEILING THE LAWS OF ETERNITY

This book is a window into the mind of our loving God, who encourages us to grow into greater angels. It reveals His deepest intentions, answering the timely question of why He conceived such a colorful medley of religions, philosophies, sciences, arts, and other forms of expression.

For a complete list of books, visit okawabooks.com

WHAT'S YOUR AIM, KIM JONG-UN?

REVEALING HIS MOST RECENT THOUGHTS

"It would be like a dream if the mass media in the world, including Japan, were permitted to conduct a completely exclusive interview with Kim Jong-un now. Although a spiritual coverage, this book realized over 70% of that wish."

-From the Preface

SPIRITUAL INTERVIEW WITH THE GUARDIAN SPIRIT OF MALALA YOUSAFZAI

A WIND OF HOPE FOR THE ISLAMIC WORLD

This is the spiritual interview with the youngest Nobel Peace Prize laureate, Malala Yousafzai's guardian spirit. Learn about where her unyeilding courage and strength springs from, and her vision that she has for the future.

DONALD TRUMP VS. KIM JONG-UN

A SPIRITUAL BATTLE BETWEEN TWO LEADERS

Who will pull the trigger first, Kim Jong-un or Donald Trump? The North Korean issue is entering the final phase. This book tells Kim Jong-un's scenario and the crucial points of Donald Trump's strategy. Here is the top-secret information to the North Korean issue.

For a complete list of books, visit okawabooks.com

SPIRITUAL INTERVIEW WITH PRINCESS DIANA

HER MESSAGES, 20 YEARS AFTER HER DEATH

This spiritual message tells us about the background of the Paris accident and what Diana has been doing since her death. Diana said that through the spiritual conversation, she was able to deepen her understanding on the Spirit World and her own soul, and that she gained the key to return to the world of goddesses in Heaven.

MARGARET THATCHER'S MIRACULOUS MESSAGE

AN INTERVIEW WITH THE IRON LADY 19 HOURS AFTER HER DEATH

Nineteen hours after Margaret Thatcher's death, Master Ryuho Okawa summoned her spirit to hold a spiritual interview. Her words will prove helpful not only to the United Kingdom, but also to the global economy and governments all over the world, including those of the United States and the European Union.

THE NEW DIPLOMATIC STRATEGIES OF SIR WINSTON CHURCHILL

A SPIRITUAL INTERVIEW WITH THE FORMER PRIME MINISTER REGARDING THE AGE OF PERSEVERANCE

If there is a chance to hear the opinion of Sir Winston Churchill on current international affairs, journalists around the world will probably be interested to hear this. This book made this possible.

For a complete list of books, visit okawabooks.com

Spiritual Interview with Liu Xiaobo

The Fight for Freedom Continues

On July 21, 2017, 8 days after his death, the spirit of Liu Xiaobo was resurrected to deliver his messages. This book reveals the truths about China, a totalitarian country that doesn't grant freedom to its people. In this book, the Chinese Nobel Prize winner shares his wish to hand down the movement of China's democratization to future generations.

Steve Jobs Returns with His Secrets

Be Simple, Be Crazy

In this spiritual interview with Steve Jobs, conducted just three months after his death, Master Okawa offers us a chance to catch a glimpse into the mind of one of America's modern geniuses, such as the aesthetic philosophy behind his passionate drive to create products, and the secrets to his creativity.

Nelson Mandela's Last Message

A Conversation with Madiba
Six Hours After His Death

As Mandela's spirit says in this spiritual interview, God created us as thinking energy and that our colorless soul is the basis of our fundamental freedom and equality. You will get a glimpse into the mind of this great leader whose undefeated spirit is a message of hope to us all.

For a complete list of books, visit okawabooks.com

THE LAWS OF WISDOM
SHINE YOUR DIAMOND WITHIN

This book guides you along the path on how to acquire wisdom, so that you can break through any wall you are facing or will confront in your life or in your business. You will lean how to go beyond the level of just amassing knowledge. It will help you come up with many great ideas, make effective planning and strategy and develop your leadership skills.

THE LAWS OF PERSEVERANCE
REVERSING YOUR COMMON SENSE

"No matter how much you suffer, the Truth will gradually shine forth as you continue to endure hardships. Therefore, simply strengthen your mind and keep making constant efforts in times of endurance, however ordinary they may be. "

-From the Postscript

THE LAWS OF HOPE
THE PATH TO YOUR DREAM, SUCCESS, AND MISSION IN LIFE

This book offers various simple tips to find happiness: how to overcome depressed feelings and live happily; how to improve your relationships; how to choose a good life partner; how to achieve your dreams; and how to achieve success in your private life and in your business. By practicing these tips, you can find hope in your future and you, yourself, will be the light to illuminate the world.

For a complete list of books, visit okawabooks.com

INVINCIBLE THINKING
AN ESSENTIAL GUIDE FOR A LIFETIME OF GROWTH, SUCCESS, AND TRIUMPH

The principles of invincible thinking in this book will allow you to achieve long-lasting triumph. This powerful and unique philosophy is not only about becoming successful or achieving our goal in life, but also about building the foundation of life that becomes the basis of our life-long, lasting success and happiness.

THE LAWS OF GREAT ENLIGHTENMENT
ALWAYS WALK WITH BUDDHA

We often find ourselves unable to forgive someone and maintain a peaceful mind. However, there are ways to lead a stress-free life and enjoy happiness from within. By understanding the Buddhist concept of "enlightenment" in this book, you will gain the power to forgive sins and get to know how to be the master of your own mind.

THE MYSTICAL LAWS
GOING BEYOND THE DIMENSIONAL BOUNDARIES

"I believe that once you have finished reading this book, you will find it impossible to return to your old self, for you have now learned the secrets that run through this world and the other.
-From the Afterword

For a complete list of books, visit okawabooks.com

MUSIC BY RYUHO OKAWA

El Cantare Ryuho Okawa Original Songs

A song celebrating Lord God

A song celebrating Lord God,
the God of the Earth,
who is beyond a prophet.

The Water Revolution

English and Chinese version

For the truth and happiness of
the 1.4 billion people in China
who have no freedom. Love,
justice, and sacred rage of God
are on this melody that will
give you courage to fight to
bring peace.

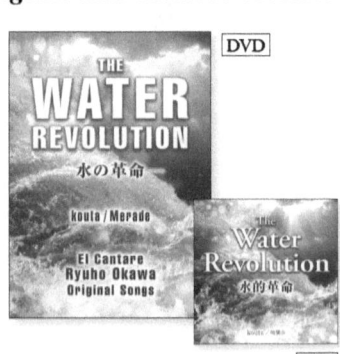

Search on YouTube

the water revolution 🔍 for a short ad!

Listen now today!

 Download from
Spotify **iTunes** **Amazon**

DVD, CD available at amazon.com,
and Happy Science locations worldwide

With Savior *English version*

This is the message of hope to the modern people who are living in the midst of the Coronavirus pandemic, natural disasters, economic depression, and other various crises.

Search on YouTube

with savior for a short ad!

The Thunder

a composition for repelling the Coronavirus

We have been granted this music from our Lord. It will repel away the novel Coronavirus originated in China. Experience this magnificent powerful music.

Search on YouTube

the thunder composition

for a short ad!

The Exorcism

prayer music for repelling Lost Spirits

Feel the divine vibrations of this Japanese and Western exorcising symphony to banish all evil possessions you suffer from and to purify your space!

Search on YouTube

the exorcism repelling

for a short ad!

Listen now today!

Download from
Spotify iTunes Amazon

DVD, CD available at amazon.com,
and Happy Science locations worldwide